Level 2

# The Nature Kid's Guide to SCORPIONS

DAVID ANDERSON

LP Media Inc. Publishing


For information address LP Media Inc. Publishing,
30012 Variolite St NW, Princeton MN 55371
www.lpmedia.org

Publication Data

Scorpions
The Nature Kid's Guide to Scorpions — First edition.

Summary: "Learn all about Scorpions, the Nature Kid Way"
— Provided by publisher.

ISBN: 979-8-89818-225-0

[1. Scorpions – Non-Fiction] I. Title.

Title: The Nature Kid's Guide to Scorpions

# CONTENTS

# DESERT DWELLERS

DID YOU KNOW?

A scorpion can hold its breath underwater for up to two days!

**Crunch! A scorpion pushes deep into the dry desert sand.**

Scorpions love hot, dry places. Most of them live in deserts, where they hide under rocks and in sandy holes.

The ground gets very hot during the day. It can reach 150 degrees! Scorpions stay cool in **burrows** below the surface. They wait there until night comes.

The Giant Desert Hairy Scorpion makes its home in the deserts of the southwest United States . It digs down deep to beat the heat. This big scorpion is one of the largest kinds in North America.

# WORLD WIDE

FUN FACT!

There are about 2,500 different kinds of scorpions on Earth — and scientists keep finding more!

## Skitter! A Deathstalker scorpion races across a sandy dune at night.

Scorpions live on six of the seven **continents**. You can find them in Africa, Asia, and the Americas. They even live in parts of Europe.

The Deathstalker lives in the deserts of North Africa and the Middle East. It is one of the most famous scorpions in the world. Its pale yellow color helps it blend in perfectly with sand.

Only Antarctica has no scorpions. It is far too cold and icy there. But almost everywhere else on Earth, scorpions call it home.

# BIG AND SMALL

The smallest scorpion in the world is less than half an inch long — smaller than a jellybean!

## Thump! An Emperor scorpion scurries across a desert rock.

Scorpions come in many sizes. Some are as small as a paper clip. Others grow as long as a ruler!

The Emperor Scorpion is one of the biggest. It can grow up to eight inches long — about the size of a banana. Despite its large size, this gentle giant rarely stings.

Most scorpions are much smaller. Many measure just two to three inches, about the length of a kid's pinky finger. Their small size helps them squeeze into tiny hiding spots.

# STINGER STYLE

**DID YOU KNOW?**

A scorpion is not a bug — it is an arachnid, related to spiders and ticks!

**Whip! A scorpion curls its tail up, ready to strike fast.**

A scorpion has three main body parts. It has a head, a middle, and a long tail that curves up and over its back.

At the end of the tail is a sharp stinger. Up front, scorpions have two big **pincers**. They use them like hands to grab and crush things.

The Arizona Bark Scorpion has a thin, curved tail and eight legs. A hard shell covers its whole body like armor. This shell protects it from enemies and stops its body from drying out in the desert heat.

# SUPER SENSORS

**FUN FACT!**

Scorpions can pick up smells using special comb-like parts on their belly!

## Shh! A scorpion feels a beetle walking ten feet away.

Scorpions have amazing senses. Small hairs on their body feel tiny movements in the air. This helps them find food in total darkness.

Most scorpions have up to twelve eyes! But they still cannot see very well. They rely on touch and vibrations much more than sight.

The Giant Desert Hairy Scorpion has hairs all over its legs and pincers. These pick up little shakes in the ground. A bug walking nearby sends signals the scorpion can feel.

# VENOM POWER

Only about 25 kinds of scorpions have venom strong enough to harm people — most are harmless to humans!

DID YOU KNOW?

## Zap! A scorpion stings a lizard that got too close.

Scorpions use venom to stay safe. When danger is near, they curl their tail up high. Then they strike fast!

The venom comes from the tip of the stinger. It can stop small animals in their tracks and keeps bigger enemies away. Most scorpions would rather run than fight.

The Deathstalker has some of the strongest venom of all scorpions. But even this fierce scorpion tries to escape first. It only stings when there is no other way out.

# BUG BUFFET

DID YOU KNOW?

When food gets scarce, some scorpions eat other scorpions!

## Munch! A hungry Emperor scorpion eats a crunchy beetle for dinner.

Scorpions eat many kinds of bugs. Crickets, beetles, and spiders are their favorite meals. They will munch on almost anything they can catch.

Bigger scorpions go after bigger food. Some eat small lizards or even mice! The Emperor Scorpion can tackle large insects with its powerful pincers.

Scorpions do not need to eat very often. But when they do, they can eat a lot. After one big meal, a scorpion's body can stretch to nearly twice its normal size!

GRAB IT

## Snap! Two strong pincers grab a spider before it can run.

Scorpions are patient hunters. They sit very still and wait. When a bug walks by, they pounce!

First, a scorpion grabs its meal with its pincers. Then it stings the **prey** to stop it from struggling. After that, it settles in for a nice long feast.

The Fat-tailed Scorpion has a thick, powerful tail. It can take down big prey with one quick sting. This makes it one of the fastest and most skilled hunters in the scorpion world.

**Scorpions turn their food into liquid and sip it like soup — a meal can take hours to finish!**

# WATCH OUT

DID YOU KNOW?

Grasshopper mice are immune to scorpion venom — they gobble scorpions up like candy!

**Scurry! A scorpion senses a Fennec Fox coming and darts into its burrow.**

Even tough scorpions have enemies. Owls hunt them at night when both are active. Foxes dig them out of burrows. Lizards snatch them in the heat of the day. Some bats have even learned to pluck scorpions off rocks mid-flight before they can raise their tail.

Meerkats are the most impressive scorpion hunters of all. They have built up a resistance to scorpion venom over thousands of years, so a sting barely bothers them. They bite the stinger off first anyway — just to be safe — then eat the rest without a second thought.

# HIDE FAST

FUN FACT!

Scorpions can squeeze into a crack as thin as a credit card!

## Whoosh! A scorpion slips into a thin crack in the rock wall.

Scorpions are masters at hiding from danger. They can slip into tiny spaces between rocks. Their flat bodies help them fit in spots that seem impossible.

The Flat Rock Scorpion is built for hiding. Its body is very thin and wide, almost like a pancake. It slides into cracks that no other animal can reach.

Once hidden, a scorpion can be very hard to find. It does not move or make a sound. It waits perfectly still until the danger passes.

# SCUTTLE SPEED

DID YOU KNOW?

Some scorpions can walk upside down on the underside of rocks and branches!

## Tap, tap, tap! Eight small legs race across the hot sand.

Scorpions scurry fast on the ground. They dart across sand and rocks with ease. Their legs grip well, even on steep slopes.

Most scorpions run in quick bursts. They sprint to catch prey or escape danger, then stop and hold perfectly still. This stop-and-go style confuses enemies.

The Deathstalker is one of the fastest scorpions around. It can zip across the sand in a flash. Its speed helps it chase down bugs and escape from hungry birds.

# NIGHT LIFE

DID YOU KNOW?

A scorpion can spend almost its whole life sitting in one spot — some barely move for months!

## Rustle! A scorpion creeps out of its den as the moon rises.

Scorpions are **nocturnal**. That means they love the night! While we sleep, they are wide awake and busy.

When the sun sets, scorpions come alive. They look for food and water in the cool darkness. The night air feels just right for their bodies.

The Arizona Bark Scorpion wakes up after dark to hunt for bugs under the stars. By morning, it is back in its hiding spot, resting until the next night comes.

# LONER LIFE

**FUN FACT!** A scorpion will sting any stranger that enters its burrow — even another scorpion!

## Scratch! A lone scorpion digs a burrow just for itself.

Most scorpions like to be alone. They do not live in groups or packs. Each one has its own hiding spot and guards it fiercely.

If two scorpions meet, they may fight. They wave their pincers and raise their tails high. Usually, one will back down and walk away before anyone gets hurt.

But the Emperor Scorpion is different. It can live peacefully with other scorpions in one burrow. A small family group may share the same cozy home.

# DANCE DATE

FUN FACT!

The scorpion dance is called a 'promenade à deux' — French for 'a walk for two'!

## Swish! Two scorpions lock pincers and start a special dance.

When a male scorpion finds a female, they dance! The male grabs her pincers with his. Then he leads her back and forth in a slow, careful walk.

This dance can last for hours. The male moves her around very gently, searching for just the right spot. One wrong move could end the dance early.

Flat Rock Scorpions do this dance on rocky ledges high above the ground. The male must be extra careful not to slip. It is one of nature's most unusual courtship rituals.

# TINY TOTS

DID YOU KNOW?

A baby scorpion sheds its skin up to seven times before it reaches adult size!

## Pop! A tiny white baby scorpion is born right from its mom.

Baby scorpions do not hatch from eggs. They are born alive, just like puppies! A mother can have many babies at once — sometimes over 100.

The babies are tiny and white. Their soft bodies have no hard shell yet, so they cannot protect themselves. They need their mother's help to survive.

Fat-tailed Scorpion babies are very small at birth. They grow slowly over many months, shedding their skin as they get bigger. It takes years for them to be fully grown.

# PIGGYBACK RIDE

DID YOU KNOW

If a baby falls off its mother's back, she stops and waits for it to climb back on!

## Scritch! Baby scorpions scramble up onto their mother's back.

Scorpion babies climb onto their mom's back right after birth. She carries all of them at once! They hold on tight with their tiny legs and pincers.

The mother keeps her young safe from danger. She does not eat while she carries them. For about two weeks, they ride everywhere she goes.

Emperor Scorpion moms are especially good parents. They keep their little ones close and warm. When the babies are big enough, they climb off and start their own lives.

# ANCIENT ARMOR

**DID YOU KNOW?**

Some scorpions can survive being frozen solid in ice — and walk away when they thaw!

## Howl! Wind blows hard, a scorpion ducks back into its burrow.

Scorpions are one of the oldest animals on Earth. They have been around for over 400 million years. That is even older than dinosaurs!

Their tough shell keeps them safe from heat and cold. Scorpions can go without food for a whole year by slowing their bodies down to save energy. They are true survival experts.

Scorpions can live through burning sun, freezing nights, and months without rain. They have lasted this long because they are so tough and adaptable.

# SAFE SPOTTING

FUN FACT!

Scientists still do not know why scorpions glow under UV light!

## Flick! On goes a UV light, and a scorpion glows bright green.

Looking for scorpions at night is one of the coolest nature adventures you can have. All you need is a UV flashlight. Shine it on the ground and rocks around you and any scorpion nearby will suddenly glow a brilliant blue-green in the darkness.

Move slowly and quietly. Scorpions sense vibrations in the ground, so heavy footsteps can send them hiding before you spot them.

Always watch from a safe distance and never try to touch one. Bring a grown-up along and have fun scorpion hunting!

# GLOSSARY

**burrow**

A hole or tunnel an animal digs to live in.

**continent**

One of the seven large land areas on Earth.

**nocturnal**

Active at night and sleeping during the day.

**pincers**

The claw-like parts a scorpion uses to grab things.

**prey**

An animal that another animal hunts for food.

www.ingramcontent.com/pod-product-compliance
Lightning Source LLC
LaVergne TN
LVHW071209160826
845679LV00003B/779
*9798898182250*